STRENGTHENING LOCAL GOVERNMENT ENGAGEMENT IN THE GREATER MEKONG SUBREGION

A STRATEGIC APPROACH

NOVEMBER 2024

CONTENTS

TABLE AND FIGURE

TABLE

FIGURE

ACKNOWLEDGMENTS

This report was prepared by Pradeep Srivastava (lead consultant) and supervised by Asadullah Sumbal, principal regional cooperation specialist, Regional Cooperation and Integration (RCI) Unit, Southeast Asia Regional Department (SERD), Asian Development Bank (ADB) (unit head, Greater Mekong Subregion [GMS] Secretariat) under the overall guidance of Alfredo Perdiguero, regional director and head of the RCI Unit, SERD, ADB. Valuable support, cooperation, and guidance were provided by the GMS National Secretariats and selected local government representatives from Cambodia, the People's Republic of China (PRC), the Lao People's Democratic Republic (Lao PDR), Thailand, and Viet Nam, including the Council for the Development of Cambodia (Cambodia), the Ministry of Planning and Investment (Lao PDR), the Ministry of Finance (PRC), the Ministry of Commerce (PRC), the Office of the National Economic and Social Development Council (Thailand), and the Ministry of Planning and Investment (Viet Nam), along with the stakeholders who participated in the consultation meeting in Bangkok on 20 October 2023 and bilateral country consultations during February and March 2024. The report was possible with the tireless coordination and follow-up efforts by a dedicated GMS Secretariat team comprising Alma Canarejo, Josephine Duque-Comia, Maria Mendez, and Cira Rudas at the GMS Secretariat, ADB; Hoai Phan (ADB Viet Nam Resident Mission); Kheuavanh Phanthaboun (ADB Lao PDR Resident Mission); Chanchamnap Sok (ADB Cambodia Resident Mission); and Yajunzhi Zhong (ADB PRC Resident Mission).

ABBREVIATIONS

ADB	Asian Development Bank
CMGF	Chief Ministers and Governors' Forum
ECD	economic corridors development
ECF	Economic Corridors Forum
GCMC	Green Cities Mayor Council
GMS	The Greater Mekong Subregion
GMS-2030	Greater Mekong Subregion Economic Cooperation Strategic Framework 2030
GMS Program	The Greater Mekong Subregion Economic Cooperation Program
IMT-GT	Indonesia–Malaysia–Thailand Growth Triangle
MPEs	multiple points of engagement
PRC	The People's Republic of China
RIF	Regional Investment Framework
SCF	sub-corridor forums
SOM	senior officials meeting
UN	United Nations

EXECUTIVE SUMMARY

The Greater Mekong Subregion (GMS) Economic Cooperation Program (GMS Program) was established in 1992 with Cambodia, the People's Republic of China (PRC, specifically the Guangxi Zhuang Autonomous Region and Yunnan Province), the Lao People's Democratic Republic (Lao PDR), Myanmar, Thailand, and Viet Nam as members. With support from the Asian Development Bank (ADB) and other development partners, the GMS Program supports the implementation of high-priority subregional projects in agriculture, energy, environment, health, tourism, transport, trade and investment facilitation, and urban development. The 7th GMS Leaders' Summit in 2021 endorsed the program's long-term strategy: the *Greater Mekong Subregion Economic Cooperation Strategic Framework 2030* (GMS-2030). GMS-2030 called for increased engagement of the GMS Program with its diverse stakeholders, including local governments.

This report outlines strategies to strengthen local government engagement in the GMS Program. The report is based on review, analysis, and experience of the GMS Program structure and activities, as well as extensive stakeholder consultations. Three crosscutting innovation areas of GMS-2030 are closely linked to local government engagement: GMS as an open platform, enhanced spatial approach, and increased dialogue and capacity building. Local government participation will also enhance the application of the principle of subsidiarity by the GMS Program, which promotes local governance for tasks best handled at the local level. Local authorities are well placed to understand the development needs of their residents—including the most vulnerable—and are in direct contact.

The Economic Corridors Forum (ECF) and the Governors' Forum are the key mechanisms for local government engagement in the GMS. However, awareness and participation of local governments in these forums remain low, limiting the effectiveness and inclusivity of the program. Existing engagements have not adequately addressed localized challenges or promoted spatially targeted economic corridor development.

Strategic recommendations to strengthen local government engagement with the GMS Program are:

(i) **Utilize existing mechanisms.** The ECF's flexible design, mandate, and history make it an ideal platform to enhance local government engagement. Continue leveraging oversight and guidance from the GMS national secretariats for local government engagement to ensure suitable country participation.

(ii) **Continue strengthening the Governors' Forum for inclusivity and visibility.** Increase inclusivity by aligning the Governors' Forum structure and content with the capacities and interests of a broader set of local governments and by advancing the presentation of themes and agendas to the GMS member countries. At the same time, the visibility of the Governors' Forum should rise with increased coordination with the ECF.

(iii) **Strengthen the ECF into a platform with inclusive, multiple points of engagement with local governments, including sub-corridor forums.** The multiple points of engagement will initially include smaller gatherings of provincial and other local stakeholders focused on the development of spatially targeted subsegments of the GMS economic corridors. The sub-corridor forums (SCFs) may also cover border-linked local governments. Outcomes and proceedings of these SCFs will be reported to the ECF for follow up. The SCFs should have clearly defined objectives, foster private sector engagement, and avoid rigid institutionalization. The GMS Program should pilot one SCF each in early 2025 and 2026.

(iv) **Invite local governments to play a more significant role in the Regional Investment Framework and the GMS working groups.** Encourage local governments to actively participate in programming and project implementation by involving them in the Regional Investment Framework and sector working groups.

(v) **Include city local governments in the ECF, Governors' Forum, and SCFs.**

(vi) **Expand development partners' role in the ECF and Governors' Forum.**

(vii) **Boost local government capacity building.** This will also enhance the quality of local government engagement.

1

INTRODUCTION

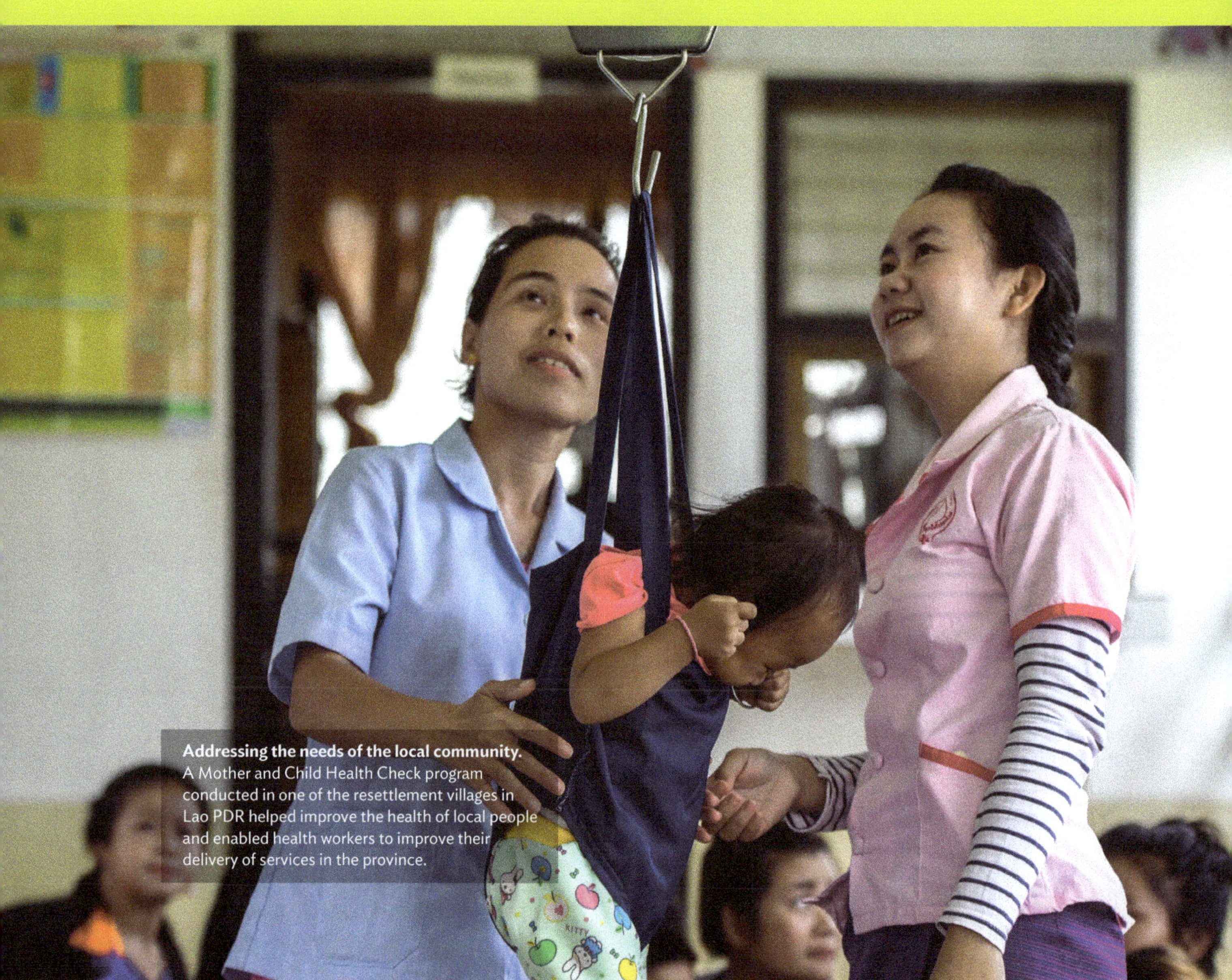

Addressing the needs of the local community.
A Mother and Child Health Check program conducted in one of the resettlement villages in Lao PDR helped improve the health of local people and enabled health workers to improve their delivery of services in the province.

The Greater Mekong Subregion (GMS) Economic Cooperation Program (GMS Program) was established in 1992. Its members are Cambodia, the People's Republic of China (PRC, specifically the Guangxi Zhuang Autonomous Region and Yunnan Province), the Lao People's Democratic Republic (Lao PDR), Myanmar, Thailand, and Viet Nam.[1] The GMS Program is a subregional economic cooperation program designed to enhance economic relations. It is founded upon the premise that regional cooperation can be a powerful development accelerator that can facilitate its members' development.

With support from the Asian Development Bank (ADB) and other development partners, the GMS Program supports the implementation of high-priority subregional projects in agriculture, energy, environment, health, tourism, transport, transport and trade facilitation, and urban development. Since 1992, GMS projects have achieved substantial progress for the program. Projects have focused on increasing connectivity through the development of physical infrastructure and economic corridors; improving competitiveness through the facilitation of cross-border movement of goods; more efficient tourism, agriculture, and urban sectors; and building a greater sense of community by working together on shared concerns in terms of health and the environment.

Local governments can be the primary body that understands local needs.

As part of its continuing robust implementation of the *Greater Mekong Subregion Economic Cooperation Strategic Framework 2030* (GMS-2030), the program assessed its engagement with local governments and explored mechanisms to strengthen partnerships with them.[2] The 7th GMS Leaders' Summit in 2021 set the vision to develop "a more integrated, prosperous, sustainable, and inclusive subregion," the implementation of which would require the GMS Program to transform into an "open and inclusive platform." GMS-2030 noted that this inclusivity would require more active involvement of the diverse stakeholders of the GMS Program, including local governments (ADB and GMS Secretariat 2022a).[3] This report presents the strategy to strengthen local government engagement in the GMS Program.[4]

Local government[5] participation will enhance the application of the GMS Program of the "principle of subsidiarity" into regional cooperation.[6] To promote an appropriate governance response to the needs and aspirations of all people, central governments should perform tasks that provincial or local governments cannot perform effectively.

---

[1] Effective 1 February 2021, ADB placed a temporary hold on sovereign project disbursements and new contracts in Myanmar.

[2] ADB. 2021. *The Greater Mekong Subregion Economic Cooperation Program Strategic Framework 2030.*

[3] The private sector, academia, civil society, and development partners are some of the other stakeholders. In 2022, as part of its transition to a more open platform, the program undertook a study on increasing development partner engagement in the GMS Program. The study and its recommendations were adopted by the 25th GMS Ministerial Conference in the Lao PDR in 2022. ADB, GMS Secretariat. 2022. *Deepening Development Partners' Engagement in the Greater Mekong Subregion Program.*

[4] This document was endorsed by the GMS senior officials in their meeting on 17 May 2024 in Yuxi, the PRC.

[5] The GMS countries' administrative structures are heterogeneous, with different layers of government such as provincial, sub-provincial, district, municipal, or subdistrict. Unless otherwise specified, this report views "local government" as the government administration at the level immediately below national government, which in most cases would mean provincial government.

[6] The principle of subsidiarity holds that problems should be dealt with at the most immediate (local) level that is consistent with their solution. Higher levels of government should play only a subsidiary role in facilitating solutions.

Collaboration in border regions. Bavet Checkpoint. Moc Bai, Viet Nam / Bavet, Cambodia on Route 1 to Phnom Penh—GMS Southern Economic Corridor. With streamlined policies and procedures, the border gate facilitates easier passenger crossing and cross-border trade.

Central governments may have more capacity to deliver high-level policy measures while local authorities are in direct contact with their residents, including the most vulnerable groups. They can, therefore, be the primary body to evaluate and understand the needs within their jurisdictions.[7] Greater engagement between the GMS Program and local and provincial governments can promote greater efficiency in identifying problems and needs and devising solutions at appropriate levels of government implementation.[8]

Provincial and other local governments may lack the technical capacity, financial resources, and expertise to solve local problems, especially those related to regional cooperation. National governments (with support from the GMS Program) may need to strengthen provincial and local governments. This may take the form of delegating decision-making to lower levels of government (where appropriate to the local conditions) and providing them with adequate financial and human resources. The GMS Program can help mobilize knowledge, technical expertise, and potentially financial resources to help member countries

---

[7]   The country-led design of the GMS Program also exemplifies the subsidiarity principle. National governments are the immediate locus for cooperation among countries. Since the GMS Program aims to facilitate and promote regional cooperation among countries, it is best led by the national governments, while multilateral agencies like ADB and other development partners play a subsidiary role.

[8]   The 2030 Agenda at the United Nations (UN) recognizes that localizing the Sustainable Development Goals will be crucial to accelerate their overall achievement and implementation. It calls upon governments and public institutions to work closely with regional and local authorities to consider local conditions and needs. See the UN Department of Economic and Social Affairs. Committee of Experts on Public Administration (CEPA). https://publicadministration. un.org/en/Intergovernmental-Support/Committee-of-Experts-on-Public-Administration/Governance-principles/ Addressing-common-governance-challenges/-Subsidiarity. UN. 2015. *Transforming Our World: The 2030 Agenda for Sustainable Development. Resolution Adopted by the General Assembly on 25 September 2015.*

improve the role and engagement of the local and provincial governments in regional development challenges.

The GMS Secretariat presented an initial concept note at the 12th GMS Economic Corridors Forum in November 2021.[9] The GMS senior officials meeting (SOM) in April 2023 reviewed a draft that outlined the strategic framework and highlighted significant issues to be addressed. The GMS Secretariat developed the report further through desk research, a review and analysis of the GMS Program's structure and activities, and discussions with stakeholders. In October 2023, the GMS Secretariat presented an updated study draft to the GMS SOM and a stakeholder

The GMS Program can help mobilize knowledge, technical expertise, and potentially, financial resources to help member countries improve the role and engagement of the local and provincial governments in regional development challenges.

meeting, which included local governments from the subregion. Country and stakeholder consultations occurred in February and March 2024, and GMS senior officials endorsed the final report in May 2024 (footnote 2).

---

[9] The paper proposed holding GMS local government meetings that would identify needs and challenges for regional cooperation and integration at provincial levels, help the GMS Program identify how to address these challenges, and help enhance the interface between local leadership and the GMS Program. The local government meetings could act as a platform to facilitate dialogue between neighboring provinces, districts, and cities for strengthened cooperation. All the GMS countries welcomed the paper and provided specific feedback, such as the need to provide more capacity building for local governments and the desirability of inviting GMS governors and mayors to the proposed meetings to increase familiarization with the GMS Program.

2

UNPACKING LOCAL GOVERNMENT ENGAGEMENT

Capacity building activities. Consultation and training program in a resettlement village near the Nakai Reservoir, at the he Nam Theun 2 hydropower plant in the Lao PDR.

It is useful to consider potential forms and modalities of local government engagement and what may be the resulting benefits of different initiatives. Not all types of local government engagement would have uniform benefits and impacts, and their costs would also vary with regard to financial and administrative resources. The table outlines the most common rationale and benefits of local government engagement that would be relevant to the GMS Program. The last column assesses the likely impact, which may vary across different types of engagement.

Rationale and Benefits of Local Government Participation in the Greater Mekong Subregion Program

No.	Rationale/Engagement	Remarks	Likely Benefit Impact
1	Improved ability of local governments to identify needs at ground level can lead to effective and efficient bottom-up project development	Consistent with the subsidiarity principle. Assumes local governments have relevant technical capacity to translate proximity to issues into better understanding and identifying the "right" projects (solutions). Bottom-up project development is useful as it can help bridge gaps in national project planning and programming process.	Likely high with improved technical and knowledge capacity of the local government. Otherwise, moderate.
2	Monitoring project implementation at local or provincial levels	Likely not useful for hard infrastructure projects with tangible and easily visible progress milestones. May be more useful in social sector projects and soft infrastructure (trade facilitation, health services, primary and secondary schools, urban services) that require more monitoring.	Low to moderate.
3	Diversity of ideas and opinions, innovative inputs	The problem set and experience of provincial and local government are diverse, from central government to each other. Even without intensive capacity building at local and provincial government levels, this diversity can contribute to innovations, identifying new and emerging issues and new ways of looking at old problems.	High.
4	Disseminating information about GMS opportunities (e.g., for capacity building, knowledge sharing opportunities, GMS Regional Investment Framework, and ongoing projects with expected localized impacts)	Will be facilitated by greater familiarity with the GMS Program but will need initiative and resources from the program for implementation.	Since an expanded information frontier can greatly enhance opportunities for local citizens, impact can be moderate to high.

Continued on next page

Table continued

No.	Rationale/Engagement	Remarks	Likely Benefit Impact
5	Boosting private sector engagement	Central policies mostly drive the business climate and private investment environment. However, local authorities can make a difference in local clearances, quality of life in their jurisdictions, negotiating incentives with the central government, and other ways depending upon the delegation of authority and local conditions in the country.	Depending upon local conditions, local and provincial governments can significantly determine factors that attract private capital, such as security and safety, children's schooling, and urban services. The likely benefit impact of increased local government engagement in promoting private sector engagement in their jurisdictions is therefore expected to be moderate to high.
6	Improved efficiency of managing links between urban development, climate change and environment, and digitalization: green, smart, and sustainable cities	Rapid and large-scale urbanization in the GMS and rapid technical change have been recognized as priority areas in GMS-2030. Governments have also prioritized these issues, focusing on smart and green cities that successfully manage the climate footprint of dense populations and economic activities.	The urgency of managing rapid urbanization, climate change, and harnessing technology means stronger engagement between cities, and the GMS Program could potentially have impact that may be rated high, even transformational.

GMS = Greater Mekong Subregion, GMS-2030 = Greater Mekong Subregion Economic Cooperation Strategic Framework 2030.
Source: Developed by the GMS Secretariat.

The table highlights how increased local government participation in the GMS Program can have highly beneficial impacts. Aside from the possibility of local and provincial government involvement in monitoring projects implemented, all other rationales and benefits are likely strong, particularly for contributing to innovations through the exchange of new ideas and approaches, boosting private sector investment and development, and managing the crucial and growing nexus of urbanization, climate change, and digitalization. The table also indicates the importance of capacity building for local and provincial governments, which can lead to a highly beneficial impact from greater engagement of these governments in the GMS Program, including identifying and helping design projects for the RIF (ADB and GMS Secretariat 2022b).[10]

> **Local government participation in the GMS Program can have highly beneficial impacts, particularly for contributing to innovations through the exchange of new ideas and approaches, boosting private sector investment and development, and managing the crucial and growing nexus of urbanization, climate change, and digitalization.**

---

[10] The RIF is a pipeline of near-term priority projects that align with the strategies, goals, and thematic priorities set in GMS-2030. The RIF focuses on mobilizing project financing with a 3-year rolling pipeline, which is extended forward each year with updated projects added or dropped from the pipeline. ADB, GMS Secretariat. 2022. *Regional Investment Framework 2023–2025*.

Encouraging private sector investment. A flower shop in Chiang Rai, Thailand. GMS Route 3 provided opportunities for locals to increase income.

3

FRAMEWORK: GMS-2030 AND LOCAL GOVERNMENT ENGAGEMENT

Economic implications of regional connectivity initiatives. Can Tho City, Viet Nam, an economic center of the Mekong Delta and an important transport hub between provinces in the region.

The strategic approach addresses the issue of local government engagement with the GMS Program within the context of GMS-2030 approved by the GMS leaders. GMS-2030 identified six crosscutting areas of innovation as key to the new GMS mission, of which three are directly linked to increasing engagement of local governments in the program: (i) transforming GMS Program into an open platform; (ii) using an enhanced spatial approach in GMS operations; and (iii) fostering dialogue, knowledge sharing, and capacity building among key stakeholders.[11] The figure highlights the differentiated role of the three innovation priorities in any strategic approach to strengthen the engagement of local governments in the GMS Program.

The GMS as an open platform, and increased local government engagement are mutually reinforcing. As GMS-2030 noted, transforming the program into an open platform would entail increased participation of local governments. Conversely, robust engagement of local and provincial governments requires that the program transform into an open platform. In particular, the institutional structure and mechanisms of the GMS Program would

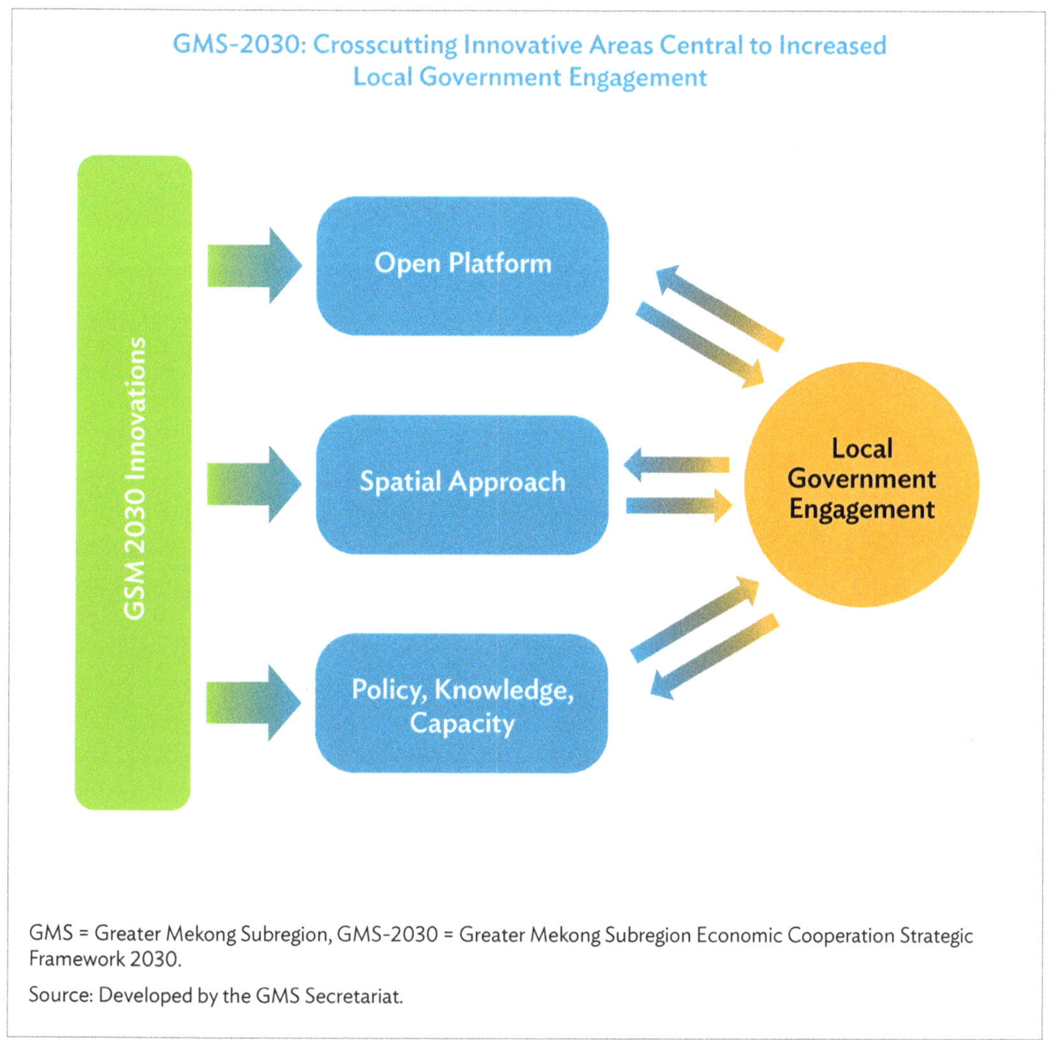

GMS = Greater Mekong Subregion, GMS-2030 = Greater Mekong Subregion Economic Cooperation Strategic Framework 2030.

Source: Developed by the GMS Secretariat.

---

[11] The remaining three innovation priority areas of GMS-2030 are (i) harnessing the digital revolution, (ii) embracing private sector solutions, and (iii) adopting a results framework for monitoring and evaluation.
A GMS-2030 Results Framework was presented for notation at the GMS Ministerial Conference in 2022.

Understanding the local industry and its interconnectedness within the region. Motorcycle tires being manufactured at the Lao Bao Commercial Area in Huong Hoa District, Quang Tri, Viet Nam.

need to incorporate greater space and role for local government engagement. This is depicted in the figure on page 9 as the two-way relationship between the GMS Program as an open platform and increased local government engagement.

A similar two-way relationship characterizes increased local government engagement and the second innovation area: adopting a spatial approach. The spatial approach of GMS-2030 emphasizes an area-based development of economic corridors integrating dynamic border areas, regional clusters of competitive cities, and their hinterland and rural areas. This would benefit local governments through their participation in the program—identifying opportunities and challenges in their geographic

areas, and playing a role in identifying and implementing economic corridor-related projects for their spatial domain. Conversely, local government engagement in the program would be more relevant from a spatial approach and area-based economic corridor development.[12]

Unlike the other two innovation areas, the third has a more unidirectional relationship with enhancing local government engagement in the short term. GMS-2030 recognizes that local governments often have significant constraints regarding knowledge, administrative, and technical capacities. Knowledge-sharing with local and provincial governments and targeted capacity building would help improve the quality and value-addition of local government

---

[12]   In contrast, for example, to issues such as trade policy, border management through trade and transport facilitation, cross-border road and railway routes, and energy trade, which are usually the domain of central government agencies.

participation in the GMS Program. Eventually, this will also lead to mutual learning as the GMS Program will learn from closer interaction with local governments, as depicted by the reverse arrow in the figure on page 9.

The figure identifies **three key pathways** that can help strengthen local government participation in the GMS Program:

(i) **Enable the design and mechanisms** of the GMS Program for greater engagement by local governments (open platform);

(ii) **Use a spatial approach linked to economic corridors development** (ECD) to integrate local government issues into the GMS Program; and

(iii) **Strengthen knowledge sharing and capacity development** targeting increased quality of, and value addition from, local government participation.

Three GMS-2030 crosscutting areas of innovation are directly linked to increasing engagement of local governments: transformation of the program into an open platform; enhanced spatial approach; and fostering dialog, knowledge sharing, and capacity building.

4

EXISTING GREATER MEKONG SUBREGION ENGAGEMENT WITH LOCAL GOVERNMENT

East–West economic corridor. Aerial view of the border checkpoint on the Lao side of the Mekong River. The second Thai–Lao Friendship Bridge is on the horizon, which connects Mukdahan Province in Thailand with Savannakhet in the Lao PDR.

Leveraging institutional mechanisms for local government engagement. The 2023 GMS Economic Corridor Governors' Forum, Yunnan, PRC (photo from the Yunnan Department of Commerce).

The Economic Corridors Forum (ECF) and the Governors' Forum are the main instruments in the GMS Program for engaging with the local governments.[13] The ECF was conceived as a high-level program platform to review and oversee the development of the GMS economic corridors.[14] The Governors' Forum under the ECF aims to unite provincial governments linked to the GMS economic corridors to enhance economic corridors development (ECD). The tasks of the ECF are the following:

(i)   Raise the profile and increase awareness of the needs and priorities of the GMS economic corridor development;

(ii) Enhance cooperation, coordination, and networking among the GMS forums, working groups, and stakeholders along the economic corridors;

(iii) Facilitate initiatives to develop the GMS economic corridors; and

(iv) Increase the involvement of local authorities and promote private sector participation and collaboration between the public and private sectors in the GMS economic corridor development.

The GMS Program has long recognized the importance of local governments, particularly in the context of ECD. From the beginning of the ECF in 2008, the program incorporated

The ECF and its associated Governors' Forum have institutionalized local government participation since 2008.

---

13   Local government officials from a host country may participate in other GMS Program meetings such as working groups or the Ministerial Conference and Summit, but this is typically on an ad hoc basis.

14   Specifically, the ECF was established in June 2008 to facilitate the transformation of priority GMS transport corridors into economic corridors.

The design of the ECF and Governors' Forum should boost inclusivity, enhance visibility, and better address localized challenges and opportunities for spatially targeted ECD.

the Governors' Forum as an integral part of the ECF to institutionalize local government participation in economic corridor initiatives. The ECF and the Governors' Forum have since remained a regular and important part of the program.

Since 2015—while the ECF has continued to rotate among countries—the Governors' Forum is hosted annually in Kunming, Yunnan Province, PRC. The Ministry of Commerce of the Government of the PRC and the Department of Commerce of the Yunnan government support the Governors' Forum, reflecting increased program ownership by the GMS member countries. Various changes have been introduced to the Governors' Forum, such as having different types of sessions in addition to a roundtable and allowing greater flexibility in content. Stakeholder consultations expressed strong support for the goals and objectives of the Governors' Forum and appreciation for its continued valuable contributions.

As shown in the map, the GMS economic corridors cumulatively cover thousands of kilometers in terms of the transport spines. Each corridor has a distinct economic geography in its areas with distinct development challenges and opportunities. In promoting ECD, the GMS ECF has tended to be relatively high-level to encompass the vast scale and scope of the economic corridors network. This has given the ECF advantages, such as bringing attention to issues such as transport and trade facilitation at border crossings of the corridors. Conversely,

the ECF has been less successful in adequately focusing on spatially targeted, smaller areas to promote the ECD, making participation of local governments more inclusive, and highlighting local constraints and challenges to promote targeted segments of the vast economic corridors network.

To address these gaps, in 2010, the GMS Program explored corridor-specific symposiums (for the East–West Economic Corridor, the North–South Economic Corridor, and the Southern Economic Corridor) as preparatory inputs for the third ECF in 2011. Subsequently, the program developed corridor-level development plans and monitoring frameworks. However, the large scale and coverage of the GMS corridors implied that even corridor-level focus remained insufficient to adequately engage with local governments and enable a spatially targeted ECD. This is evident in that local government awareness about the GMS Program and its economic corridors remains relatively low even after 3 decades of the program's operation. To fulfill the original aims and objectives of the ECF, the GMS Program and its ECF platform— including the Governors' Forum—need to seek greater inclusivity and more spatially targeted focus as part of their design.

During consultations, several local government participants noted their lack of familiarity with the program and the Governors' Forum. They hoped that increased GMS engagement with local governments could be more inclusive. The design and content of the Governors' Forum could be reviewed to boost further inclusivity. Relatively low awareness of the Governors' Forum among local governments indicated the lack of adequate visibility of the Governors' Forum. GMS-2030 also noted that the Governors' Forum could be reinvigorated

Greater Mekong Subregion Economic Corridors

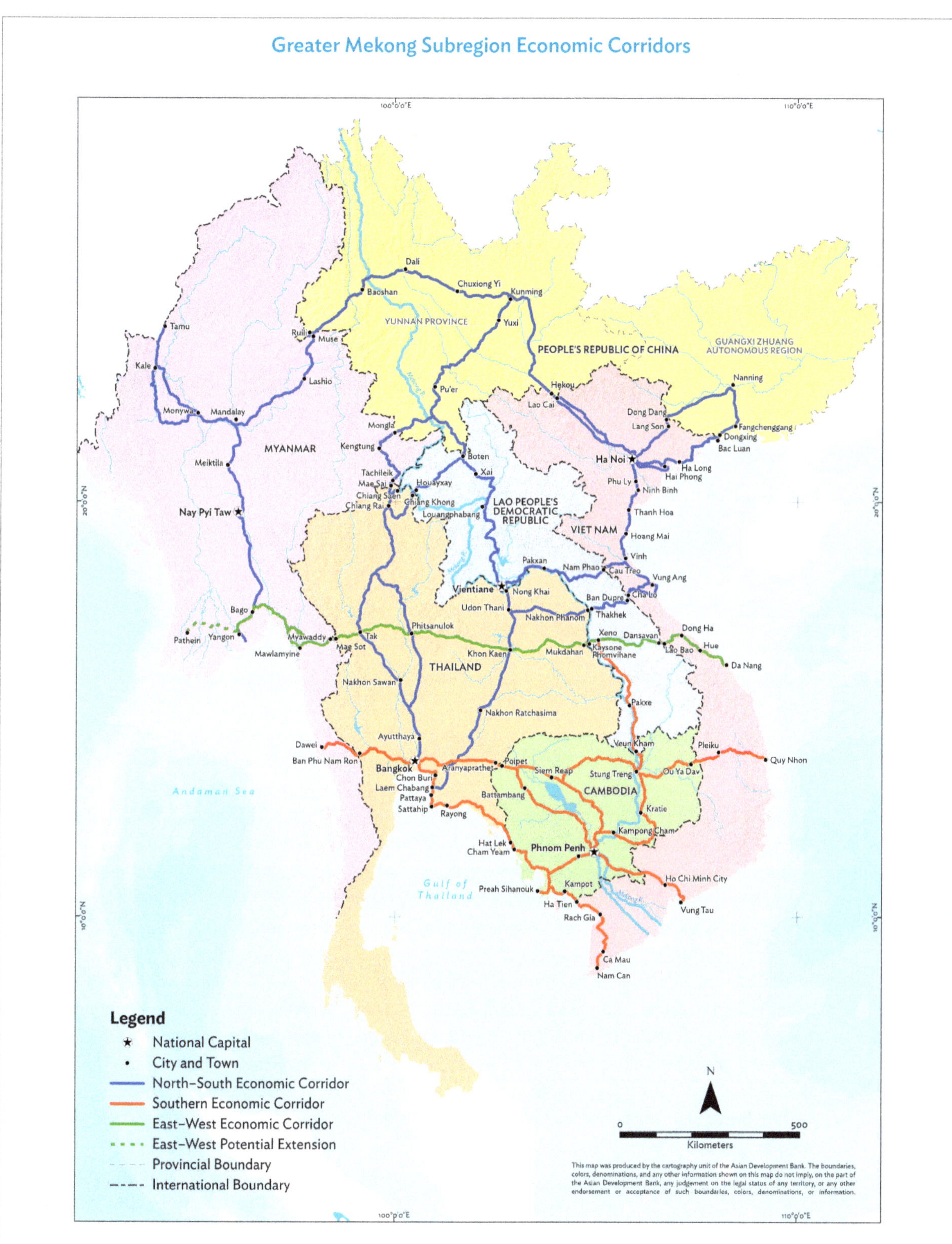

Source: ADB. 2023. *Economic Corridor Development: From Conceptual Framework to Practical Implementation – Guidance Note.* (Appendix 1). https://www.adb.org/sites/default/files/publication/913256/economic-corridor-development-guidance-note.pdf .

GMS Cross Border Transport Agreement. Customs control at the Thailand border to the Lao PDR in Mukdahan.

for more effective multisector and spatial coordination to consider provincial stakeholder interests.

Along with the Governors' Forum, the ECF design and content must be refined to enhance local government participation, consistent with GMS-2030's call to make the program more open and inclusive. The design and content of the ECF must also incorporate GMS-2030 recommendation for increased spatial focus. Given the vast scale of the GMS corridors network, an increased spatial focus for ECD would require targeting smaller segments within particular corridors rather than as a whole.

The GMS Program has done well to recognize the importance of local government engagement, particularly in the context of ECD. The ECF and its Governors' Forum have institutionalized local government participation since 2008. Most stakeholders in the program supported the goals and objectives of this mechanism for local government engagement and appreciated their contribution. However, given the vast scale of the GMS economic corridors' network, this single point of the program's engagement with local governments has constrained inclusive local government participation and not provided adequate visibility to local government engagement. The design of the ECF and Governors' Forum can also seek to better address localized challenges and opportunities for a spatially targeted ECD in partnership with relevant stakeholders.

Anchoring regional cooperation in provincial areas. A cargo ship docks at Danang Port, a vital link in the GMS East–West Economic Corridor.

5

RECOMMENDATIONS TO STRENGTHEN LOCAL GOVERNMENT PARTICIPATION

Focus on the Governors' Forum to enhance local government engagement. The 2019 GMS Economic Corridor Governors' Forum in Kunming, Yunnan, PRC (photo from the Yunnan Department of Commerce).

The strategic approach paper draws upon the analysis and review of the GMS Program, along with extensive consultations with stakeholders, to identify a few recommendations to strengthen local government engagement with the GMS Program.

RECOMMENDATION 1: Use the institutional mechanism of the ECF to enhance local government engagement.

The flexible design, broad objectives, and history of the ECF make it an ideal platform to improve local government engagement with the GMS Program. Although not a decision-making body like the SOM and the Ministerial Conference, the ECF involves high-level participation from national governments and is mandated to engage with provincial and local governments. Creating new structures or mechanisms could risk duplicating existing mechanisms and impose financial costs on the program and additional administrative and human resource burdens on the member countries.

The program will continue to employ the existing approach through the ECF to accommodate the diversity of local government structures across GMS countries. This will be done through close involvement, oversight, and guidance by national governments. Given the variations in administrative structures, delegation of responsibilities, and stakeholder compositions at provincial and local levels, this approach will ensure the identification of suitable participants based on their functional responsibilities.

Leveraging oversight and guidance from the national GMS secretariats has been effective in addressing country diversity within the ECF and the Governors' Forum, and extending this approach to smaller, spatially-targeted sub-corridor ECD forums will further enhance local government engagement within the GMS Program.

RECOMMENDATION 2: Continue strengthening the GMS Governors' Forum for inclusivity and visibility.

The structure and content of the GMS Governors' Forum will be reviewed for possible adjustments or innovations while maintaining its continuity based on existing strengths. For example, the Governors' Forum already leverages links with academia, think tanks, and the private sector, such as business associations, to develop content across various issues.

The Governors' Forum will be supported to further align its content with the capacities and interests of a broader set of local governments, increasing its contribution to local government engagement. The host of the Governors' Forum confirmed an interest in (i) increasing the openness of the Governors' Forum by inviting more participants, (ii) exploring options to deepen cooperation mechanisms, (iii) attempting to enhance capacity building through the Governors' Forum, and (iv) exploring opportunities to increase the contribution of the Governors' Forum to trade and growth in the subregion.

Some local governments suggested that participants should have a more active role in designing or selecting topics and that themes should align with key areas of regional development, ensuring relevance and impact at the local level. The Governors' Forum can facilitate this approach, which proposes themes, topics, and agendas in advance to the GMS member countries and stakeholders for feedback. This inclusive approach will increase the visibility of the Governors' Forum through progress reports and updates being provided more broadly within the GMS Program than the current practice of only to the ECF.

The GMS Secretariat will further explore the operationalization of these proposed actions with the GMS national secretariats and stakeholders to increase the inclusivity of the

Governors' Forum (organization and content) while increasing its visibility and coordination with the ECF.

The ECF is a single-point engagement approach with local governments. While it is an effective approach overall, it does display shortcomings given the vast network of GMS economic corridors and the expanding scope of the GMS Program under GMS-2030 across various sectors and themes. In addition to the annual event, the ECF will strengthen into a platform encompassing multiple points of engagement (MPEs) with local governments to foster an open, inclusive design. The MPEs will initially include smaller gatherings of provincial and other local stakeholders focused on the ECD of spatially targeted subsegments of the GMS economic corridors. Outcomes and proceedings of these smaller sub-corridor forums (SCFs) will be reported to the ECF for follow up.

SCFs to have clearly defined objectives tied to ECD. To ensure the effectiveness of the SCFs, these will have clearly defined objectives tied to ECD while avoiding duplication and rigid institutionalization. The objectives can be based on analytical and technical groundwork, with the participation of relevant provincial governments, including those from border provinces. The SCFs will serve as platforms for local governments and other stakeholders— such as the private sector—to discuss strategic, project, and other operational aspects of ECD in their areas. The SCFs will also provide a useful and effective avenue for directly engaging the local private sector with local governments and the GMS Program. It is important to not institutionalize any SCF into a fixed cycle (e.g.,

every 1–2 years) but to match their frequency and participation with the progress of the targeted ECD agenda.

The SCF objectives may include:

(i)   Formulating or validating action plans for ECD in the relevant subsection based on prior diagnostic or other assessments.
(ii) Identifying and disseminating information on ECD investment plans under implementation and in the pipeline by central and provincial governments and development partners.
(iii) Identifying and disseminating private sector views on opportunities and constraints in developing the sub-corridor segment.
(iv) Providing expert views on the policy environment affecting investment and trade in the corridor subsegment.
(v)   Assessing trade facilitation and other bilateral trade and transport issues affecting the development of the corridor subsegment (where relevant).
(vi) Collating information on the role of development partners to improve coordination and information sharing.
(vii) Developing a framework to incorporate ECD elements, trade promotion, trade facilitation, and logistics in the context of the relevant corridor subsegment.
(viii) Monitoring, evaluating, and modifying strategies and action plans developed for ECD in the relevant sub-corridor segment.
(ix) Identifying and implementing capacity development and knowledge-sharing initiatives for local governments relevant to ECD.

SCFs to focus on border-linked local governments. This is an important area of focus for the SCFs, including distinct ECD issues stemming from their proximity to borders, shared interests and challenges, regional public goods, border trade, and other coordination and cooperation matters.

Implementing local projects. Villagers attend health outreach activities covering infectious diseases including the coronavirus disease (COVID-19) in O Kandorl village, Santepheal commune, Sampovlon District, Cambodia.

Piloting two SCFs in 2025 and 2026. The GMS Program will propose piloting two SCFs in 2025 and 2026 to test this approach, focusing on segments of the North–South and Southern Economic Corridors. These pilots will be used to (i) identify lessons for effective preparation for similar local-government interactions at a small scale; (ii) identify suitable designs for these engagements, which will need to avoid a one-size-fits-all template; and (iii) fine-tune inclusive criteria for participants in the smaller events and the contents for discussion, consultation, and coordination. Details will be developed in consultation with the GMS countries.

Encourage SCF ownership by local governments. The GMS Program will explore opportunities for greater ownership of the SCFs by provincial governments. While many local governments are typically resource-constrained, there is considerable diversity among provincial governments. The program will help to identify and encourage

provincial governments to lead the SCF within their country in coordination with the GMS national secretariats and support from development partners. This may promote a more dynamic profile for that particular SCF, similar to the Governors' Forum model, though on a much smaller scale.

> **RECOMMENDATION 4: Invite local governments to play a greater role in the RIF and the GMS sector working groups.**

Local governments will be encouraged and facilitated to play an active role in the programming of the GMS Program. This will include effective coordination between the local governments and the respective GMS national secretariats in identifying and proposing inputs into the RIF (footnote 8). The local governments will also be encouraged to contribute to monitoring project implementation for projects within their geographic jurisdictions. For programming and project implementation issues, participation of local governments in relevant sector working groups will also be encouraged.

RECOMMENDATION 5: Include cities in the ECF.

Cities represent a significant gap and an important axis for developing the GMS Program's engagement with local governments. As rapid migration and urbanization reshape the landscape, the GMS is witnessing rapidly growing cities. These urban areas are increasingly the most economically dynamic areas of the countries, serving as potential hubs for a spatially oriented ECD.

The program will consider fostering the participation of cities linked to the GMS economic corridors and trade hubs in the ECF, the Governors' Forum, and SCFs. This will lead to peer learning by sharing knowledge, best practices, and experience across cities. It is relevant and useful since they often face similar problems at different points of their growth cycle. Issues such as urban governance (urban planning, spatial planning, land use management, urbanization, slum management, and urban renewal), infrastructure provision, urban transport and mobility, social inclusiveness, waste management, air and water pollution, and environmental concerns are examples of the diverse spectrum of issues that will increasingly converge between effective management of cities and ECD in the GMS.[15]

The GMS Cities and Mayors' Forum— recognizing the growing role of cities and urban centers in driving GMS cooperation. The share of the national population living in cities will continue to grow with rapid urbanization across GMS countries. This trend will extend the urban share of national economic activities and regional value chains. Urban populations are already dealing with issues of growing priority in the GMS, such as digitalization, environmental management, and regional public goods through green cities, sustainability, resilience, and smart cities agendas.

Depending upon the implementation and lessons of the MPE's design of the ECF, the program will continually assess the demand for and use of dedicated gatherings of city governments and stakeholders to strengthen local government engagement and GMS cooperation. Over the medium term, establishing the GMS Cities and Mayors' Forum will be considered. As with other MPEs, a medium-term GMS Cities and Mayors' Forum must also be based on technical and analytical preparations underlying a clear agenda and objectives.

RECOMMENDATION 6: Expand the development partner role in the ECF and the Governors' Forum.

The Governors' Forum is a good example of ownership by GMS countries. Development partner participation can further expand its effectiveness. This will complement the event by sharing knowledge, best practices, and emerging issues with local governments. The development partners have the potential to enhance the effectiveness and inclusivity, and their collaboration with the Governors' Forum can be articulated by co-sponsoring specific sessions, inviting specialists or keynote speakers, or providing tailored knowledge products to meet the particular needs of local governments in the subregion.

---

[15] ASEAN has also recognized the importance of regional cooperation at the level of cities. Some subregional cooperation programs such as the Indonesia-Malaysia-Thailand Growth Triangle (IMT-GT) have already established a platform for city governments to come together for the largest cities (Appendix 2).

Training government officials. GMS East–West Economic Corridor organic vegetable value chains. Mekong Institute, Khon Kaen, Thailand.

Given that many development partners are already involved with local governments as part of their operational activities, the program will consider leveraging their expertise to enhance the attractiveness and efficacy of the Governors' Forum. This will align with a more inclusive approach to organizing the Governors' Forum.

RECOMMENDATION 7: Boost local government capacity building.

Enhanced knowledge-sharing and targeted capacity building is another pathway for increasing local government participation in the GMS Program. Many local governments emphasized that they expected greater engagement with the GMS Program to address their need for increased capacities in strategic areas, project design and implementation, environmental issues, and fiscal management.

Local government capacity building also includes increasing local government awareness of the program and its benefits aside from finding mechanisms to include them in knowledge sharing and dissemination of knowledge products relevant to them. The program has established a knowledge network that may be helpful in this direction. Similarly, the training provided by ADB's BIG (Brunei Darussalam–Indonesia–Malaysia–Philippines East ASEAN Growth Area, Indonesia–Malaysia–Thailand Growth Triangle, and the GMS) capacity building program may also strengthen local government ability to participate effectively and actively in the broader program. Other knowledge and capacity building resources will also need to be explored, including developing member cooperation.

APPENDIXES

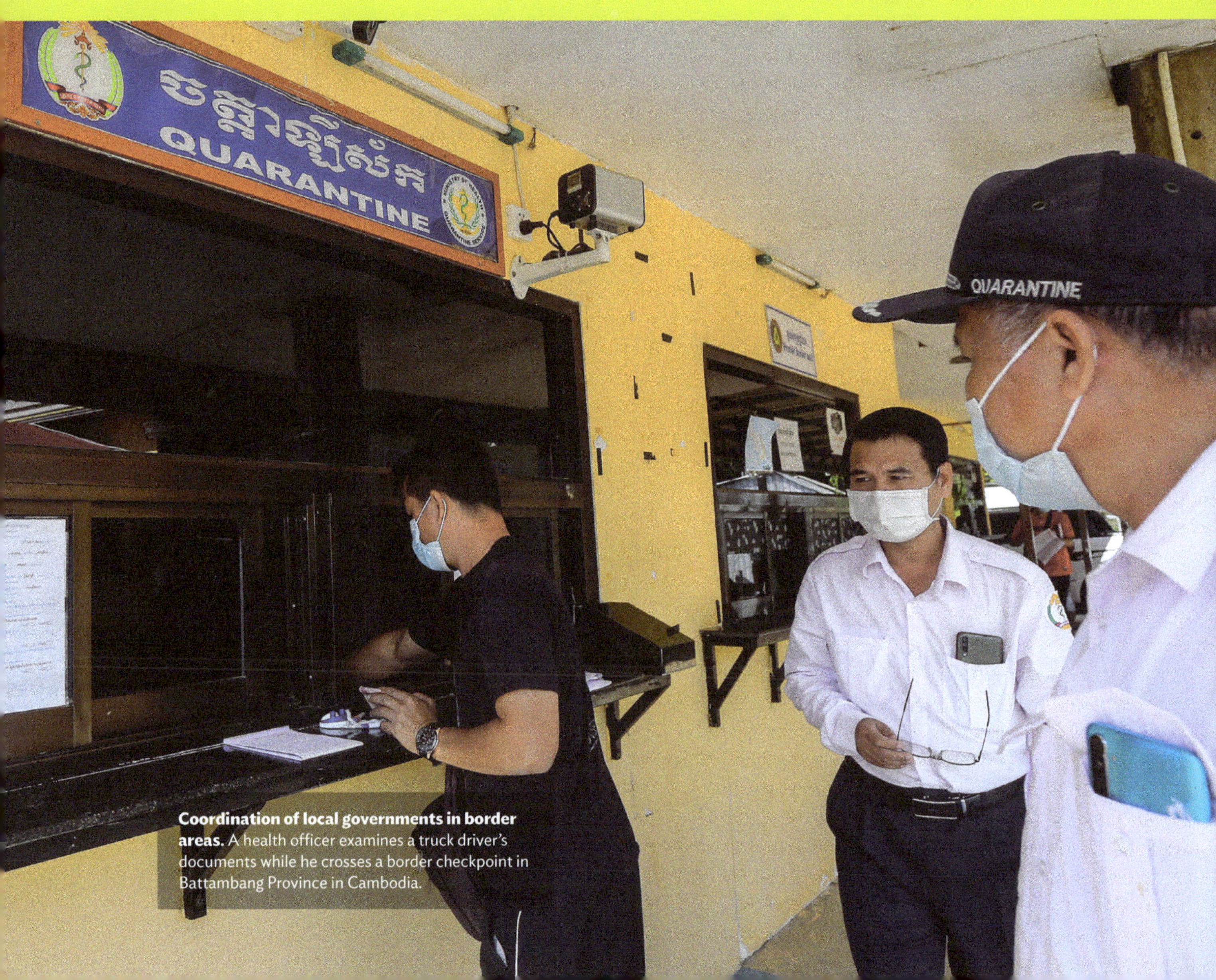

Coordination of local governments in border areas. A health officer examines a truck driver's documents while he crosses a border checkpoint in Battambang Province in Cambodia.

APPENDIX 1:

Feedback From Stakeholders' Meeting and Consultations

STAKEHOLDERS' MEETING BANGKOK, THAILAND 20 OCTOBER 2023

The day-long meeting was divided into five sessions focusing on specific aspects such as the Governors' Forum, sub-corridor forums, a city platform, and engagement points for the Greater Mekong Subregion (GMS) Program. Representatives of local governments and national secretariats from the GMS countries participated.

Most participants welcomed the goals and objectives of greater local government participation in the GMS. The local government participants were keen for greater engagement of the GMS Program with local governments due to their expectation of enhanced capacity building from such engagement. They felt engaging with the GMS Program would help local governments develop human and administrative capacities to address the diverse development challenges faced, including identifying appropriate solutions to problems, the capacity to identify, develop, and implement projects, and strengthening resource mobilization and fiscal management.

Some local government participants noted the need to adapt to national or local regulations, while others highlighted the aspirations of some cities to be regional beacons for development and cooperation. At the same time, the local government representatives fully understood the need for overall management, coordination, and oversight by the national government in their engagement with the GMS Program.

The participants were apprised of recent achievements of the Governors' Forum and expressed appreciation for its continuing achievements and contributions to GMS cooperation. Several noted that the meeting was their first introduction to the GMS and the Governors' Forum and voiced hope that the GMS would increase inclusive engagement with local governments. The design and content of the Governors' Forum could be reviewed to enhance the inclusivity and effectiveness of local governments. Relatively low awareness of the Governors' Forum among participants indicated the need to improve the visibility of the Governors' Forum for local governments in the GMS.

Participants appreciated recognizing and highlighting local issues, challenges, and opportunities for economic corridors development (ECD) in their provinces. They viewed spatially targeted smaller gatherings of provincial governments to focus on economic corridor development issues in subsegments of specific corridors and their linked provinces as helping generate customized boosts for ECD. Participating local governments felt that area-based spatial targeting would help bring visibility to ECD challenges and opportunities in their geographical territories. Local government representatives also recognized the importance of bringing together border-linked provinces with additional issues related to their border proximity. Some representatives noted that parts of the GMS economic corridors may require sub-groupings of provincial governments from as many as three countries.

Several participants noted the role of the private sector in contributing to ECD. They suggested the smaller gatherings of provincial governments could help the provinces strengthen their engagement with the local private sector while also boosting the exposure, knowledge, and capacity of the provincial private sector stakeholders.

Some local government participants underlined the importance of cities in the GMS region as hubs for promoting economic dynamism and regional cooperation. As part of the increased local government engagement, it was suggested that the GMS engage with the major drivers of growth in the region. The example of a city forum in the Indonesia–Malaysia–Thailand Growth Triangle was presented at the meeting, eliciting some suggestions that issues like green and digital cities were becoming important for all countries, including at the provincial level. Including cities in increased local government engagement by the GMS could contribute to exchanging information, strategies, and lessons on a variety of issues linked to rapid urbanization in the GMS region, such as smart or green cities, environment issues, digitalization and technology management, private sector development, and subsovereign financial mobilization.

Other Country and Local Government Consultations

Feedback from the meeting in Bangkok in October 2023 was incorporated into a revised and updated draft of the study report. This draft provided the basis for additional consultations undertaken with the GMS national secretariats and local governments during February and early March 2024. The objective was to identify any remaining issues and suggestions before finalization of the report.

While supporting increased local government engagement, countries suggested relying on existing mechanisms such as the Economic Corridors Forum (ECF) to the extent possible and not initiating new institutional structures that would entail higher costs and administrative resources from GMS and national secretariats.

All countries supported the proposal for multiple points of engagement through sub-corridor forums (SCFs) to have clearly defined objectives and agendas. Some countries reaffirmed the need for the SCFs to focus on issues relevant to trade, infrastructure, and other priorities for ECD in their provinces.

Some consultations noted the need to ensure resource mobilization is not forgotten. In particular, the suggestion was for SCFs to ensure the participation of development partners who are active in the areas and issues highlighted in the smaller forums.

All countries supported increasing the GMS Program's inclusivity in local government outreach. The heterogeneity in local government arrangements and structures was noted in the consultations. A clear agenda and objectives would also contribute to identifying the right participants in the smaller SCFs.

Some of the governments noted the existence of bilateral engagement between some of the countries at the local government level. It was noted the GMS Program could avoid overlap and duplication to ensure efficient utilization of resources.

The GMS Senior Officials' Meeting, 17 May 2024

The *Strategic Approach for Strengthening Local Governments' Engagement with the GMS Program* was tabled for review and discussion at the GSM senior officials meeting held in Yuxi, People's Republic of China, on 17 May 2024.

The countries broadly welcomed the initiative by the GMS Program to increase engagement with local governments. They agreed and underlined that the GMS Program should prioritize streamlining existing mechanisms and forums, seek greater inclusivity, and clearly define the the role of the Governors' Forum and coordination with the ECF.

The countries also appreciated the report's recommendation to optimize existing structures to enhance local government engagement to avoid creating additional or potentially duplicative mechanisms.

The senior officials meeting endorsed the *Strategic Approach for Strengthening Local Governments' Engagement with the GMS Program* in principle subject to any other written comments by 24 May 2024.

APPENDIX 2:

Local Government Participation in the Indonesia–Malaysia–Thailand Growth Triangle

The Indonesia–Malaysia–Thailand Growth Triangle (IMT-GT) is a subregional cooperation and integration program encompassing the island of Sumatra, most of Peninsular Malaysia, and selected southern provinces in Thailand.

The IMT-GT has been implementing a Chief Ministers and Governors' Forum (CMGF). According to the Implementation Blueprint 2022–26 of the IMT-GT, the CMGF's role is to work closely with the senior officials meeting (SOM) and the ministerial meeting to:[1]

(i)   Provide policy input and facilitate the implementation of the program strategy at the provincial and/or state levels.

(ii)   Sensitize local governments on the goals, objectives, strategies, programs, and projects of the IMT-GT program.

(iii)   Build awareness among local governments and businesses about the opportunities and direct and indirect benefits of IMT-GT.

(iv)   Promote bottom-up projects.

(v)   Attract private investment by leveraging investment promotion agencies operating at the state and provincial levels, coordinate with national investment promotion agencies, and offer fiscal and non-fiscal incentives (cost recovery from providing services to potential investors).

Another key role for the CMGF is overseeing green city initiatives through the **IMT-GT Green Council**. Established in 2016, the Green Council is chaired by the chief ministers or governors of member states and reports to the CMGF. The Green Council coordinates closely with the SOM to ensure high-level policy support from national governments and partner organizations (e.g., the Asian Development Bank) for advancing the IMT-GT Sustainable Urban Development Framework agenda at the subnational level.

IMT-GT further established the **Green Cities Mayor Council (GCMC)** in 2020 as the implementation arm of the Green Council, focusing on identifying, planning, managing, and implementing Sustainable Urban Development Framework projects at the subnational level. The GCMC is also mandated to take the lead in driving the implementation of the IMT-GT Green City Action Plan at the local or city level. The GCMC is supported in its work by the working group on the environment.

The induction of the green cities initiative through the Green Council and the GCMC into the CMGF provided a valuable vehicle to anchor the CMGF and clear agenda and targets.

---

[1]   Indonesia–Malaysia–Thailand Growth Triangle. Implementation Blueprint 2022–26.